FATS AND SUGARS

HEALTHY EATING

BY GEMMA McMULLEN

CONTENTS

Words that look like this can be found in the glossary on page 24.

BookLife
PUBLISHING

©2022
BookLife Publishing Ltd.
King's Lynn, Norfolk
PE30 4LS, UK

ISBN: 978-1-83927-493-0

Written by:
Gemma McMullen

Edited by:
Grace Jones

Designed by:
Ian McMullen

A catalogue record for this book is available from the British Library.

All rights reserved.
Printed in Poland.

All facts, statistics, web addresses and URLs in this book were verified as valid and accurate at time of writing. No responsibility for any changes to external websites or references can be accepted by either the author or publisher.

WHAT ARE FATS AND SUGARS?

Fat is an important part of our diet. Our bodies need small amounts of fat. We can get fats from both animals and plants. We also use fats in our cooking.

Sausages contain animal fat.

Sugar is very sweet and comes from plants. It is used to make food and drink taste sweet.

White sugar cubes

ANIMAL FATS

People sometimes eat and cook with animal fat. Some types of meat contain more fat than others.

The white streaks in bacon are fat.

Bacon

Animal fat is also used inside some food products. All of the foods below can contain animal fats.

Crisps

Chocolate

Jelly

Sweets

Vegetarians need to be careful to choose foods that do not contain any animal fats.

COOKING OILS

Cooking food in oil is called frying. Oil can also be used as an <u>ingredient</u> in cooking.

Cooking oils can be made from plants. The oil from sunflower seeds and olives is often used in cooking.

Sometimes oil is poured over food, such as salads.

BUTTER, LARD AND MARGARINE

Butter is a dairy product, meaning that it is made from milk. Butter is another type of fat that is often used in cooking.

Butter

Lard is a type of fat that comes from pigs. Margarine is sometimes made using sunflower oil. It contains less bad fats than butter and lard.

Margarine

Lard

HEALTHY FATS

We need some fat in our diet to keep us healthy. Fats give us energy and keep our skin and organs healthy. Fish, nuts, fruit and vegetables all contain healthy fats.

The healthy fats in fish, nuts and fruit give us energy.

Too much fat in our diet can be bad for our health. It is important to think about the amount of fat we eat.

Biscuits

Biscuits and pastries both contain fat.

Pastries

13

WHERE DOES SUGAR COME FROM?

Granulated sugar comes from sugarcane
or sugar beet.

Sugar cane

Granulated
sugar

Sugarcane is a type of grass that grows in warm
and wet <u>climates</u> with heavy downpours of rain.

Sugar beet is a vegetable that grows underground.

Sugar beet

HEALTHY SUGARS

It is important to have some sugar in our diet as it gives us energy. The healthiest type of sugar is natural sugar, which is often found in fruit.

Food that has sugar
added to it is not as
good for us and should
only be eaten as a treat.

Too much
sugar can be
bad for your
teeth.

HIDDEN SUGARS

We know that there is a lot of sugar in sweets and fizzy drinks, but some foods contain hidden sugars that we might not know about.

Dried fruit contains sugars.

Check labels to see how much hidden sugar might be in something.

Even <u>savoury</u> foods such as soups can contain sugar. Flavoured yoghurt, pasta sauce and even dried fruits often have sugar added to them.

TYPES OF SUGAR

Granulated sugar is usually added to drinks, such as tea and coffee, to make them sweeter.

Granulated

Caster

Caster sugar contains very small pieces of sugar. It is good for making cakes.

Sanding sugar is sprinkled on sweets and biscuits to make them look nice.

Sanding sugar

Muscovado

Muscovado sugar feels sandy, sticky and wet. It is brown in colour and can be used to sweeten coffee.

FOODY FACTS!

Avocados are high in fat.

Jam

Sugar is mixed with fruit to make jam.

Oil does not mix with water. If put together, the two will separate.

A lemon contains more sugar than a strawberry.

23

GLOSSARY

climates
the common weather of certain areas

ingredient
a food that is put with other foods to make a meal

savoury
foods that do not taste sweet

vegetarians
people who do not eat meat

INDEX

PHOTO CREDITS

Photo credits: Abbreviations: l–left, r–right, b–bottom, t–top, c–centre, m–middle. All images courtesy of Shutterstock.com. With thanks to Getty Images, Thinkstock Photo and iStockphoto. Front Cover – 1 – Ruth Black. 2 – Elena Schweitzer. 3tr, 8tr – ifong. 3br – Roman Tsubin. 4 – Joe Gough. 5 – ifong. 6 – Tobik. 6inset – Tischenko Irina. 7r – Sergiy Bykhunenko. 8br – Nikola Bilic. 9 – mama_mia. 9inset – Magdalena Kucova. 10 – Multiart. 11br – Tsekhmister.11bl – AN NGUYEN. 11mc – Ian 2010. 11inset – Viktor1. 12inset – Tina Larsson. 12 – Studio 1One. 13bl – Ruth Black. 13br – margouillat photo. 13tr – marco mayer. 14 – Nuttapong. 15inset – Nivellen77. 15, 19 – igor.stevanovic. 16 – violetkaipa. 16inset – Edward Lara. 17inset – Alena Ozerova. 17r – Sergiy Bykhunenko. 18 – zukerka. 19 – Bern James, 20tl – matin. 20tr – xavier gallego morell. 20br – 24Novembers. 21bl – Madlen. 21tr – joannawnuk. 22bl – lozas. 22br – Madlen. 22tr – Anna Kucherova. 23bl – Volosina. 23tr – Nikola Bilic. 24 – Nata-Lia. Images are courtesy of Shutterstock.com. With thanks to Getty Images, Thinkstock Photo and iStockphoto. Thank you to Denise Bentulan for use of her typeface Moonflower http://douxiegirl.com/fonts.